Sports Heroes

by Peter Weiniger

Contents

Introduction

The great thing about sports is that everyone can play them for fun, fitness, and competition.

A few children grow up to be champions. They have special talents and abilities. But just being talented isn't enough. They have to be prepared to work very hard. Swimmers get up early every morning to swim many laps in the pool before school starts. Athletes run many miles to get fit. Others work out in the gym, or practice on the tennis court, football field, or basketball court.

Champions have something else that is special: they are good sports. Good sports play fair. All the great champions in this book have this in common—they are all great athletes, and they are good sports, too.

Chapter 1

Babe Ruth

Babe Ruth is the most famous baseball player in the history of the game. His full name was George Herman Ruth, but everyone called him "Babe."

Babe Ruth was born to a poor family in Baltimore, Maryland, in 1895. He became a professional baseball player in 1914. The first team he played on was the Boston Red Sox. He won two World Series with Boston and then he joined the New York Yankees. He retired in 1935. In his last game Babe hit three home runs, and he hit the third one so hard that it flew out of the ballpark. No one had ever done that before. Baseball fans loved Babe Ruth and he loved entertaining them.

In his long career, Babe broke almost every batting record. In one season he hit 60 home runs—a record that stood for more than 30 years.

Babe Ruth died in 1948, at age 53.

Babe Ruth was a very good pitcher and batter. He won the award for hitting the most home runs in a season twelve times.

Chapter 2

Jesse Owens

American athlete, Jesse Owens, grew up on a farm. He first showed that he could run fast while he was in high school.

In 1935, when he was 22 years old, Jesse Owens broke five world records on the same afternoon. These were in the long jump, the 220 yard sprint, the 220 yard hurdles, the 200 meter sprint, and the 200 meter hurdles. He also equaled the world record for the 100 yard sprint. No one has ever done this again in such a short time.

Jesse's greatest moment came at the 1936 Olympic Games in Berlin, Germany. He won four gold medals, and he became the most popular athlete at the Games. Everywhere he went, people cheered and wanted his autograph.

Jesse Owens is still remembered as one of the greatest athletes of the 20th century.

Jesse Owens in action at the 1936 Olympics in Berlin, Germany.

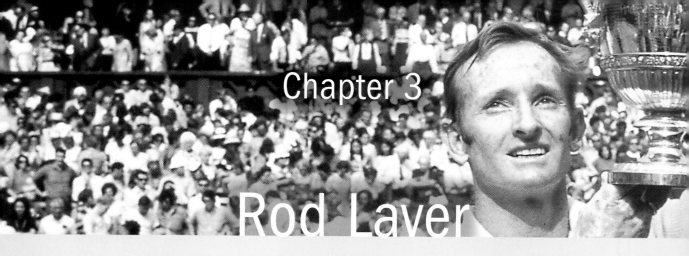

Chapter 3

Rod Laver

Australian tennis ace, Rod Laver, was noticed by a tennis coach when he was eleven years old. Because he was so small, his coach had him squeeze a tennis ball all day to strengthen his hands. Rod is left-handed, and by the time he was a teenager, his left wrist was twice as strong as his right wrist. This allowed him to hit the ball harder and spin it more sharply than his opponents.

Rod Laver's nickname was "Rocket." He won all the Grand Slam championships: Wimbledon (three times), the US Open (twice), the French Open (twice), and the Australian Open (three times). He is the only person to have won all the Grand Slam events in the same year, and he did that twice, in 1969 and 1972! He also helped his country win the Davis Cup five times. People loved to watch him play because of his skills and because he was a very fair player who never lost his temper.

Center court in Melbourne Park, the home of the Australian Open, is known as Rod Laver Arena. Rod Laver was present when the new arena was opened.

DID YOU KNOW?

Rod Laver started playing tennis on a court his father built on the family farm. His father added lights so Rod and his brothers could play at night after finishing their chores.

Chapter 4

Dawn Fraser

Australian swimming star Dawn Fraser spent most of her summer vacations playing in the local swimming pool. She was the youngest of eight children, and it was the only entertainment the family could afford.

Dawn was known for her big heart and great fighting spirit. When a swimming official told her she would never swim for Australia because her family was too poor, she became more determined to achieve her dream.

Dawn trained harder than ever. In less than two years, she broke the world record for the 100 meter *freestyle* and was chosen to represent Australia at the 1956 Olympic Games in Melbourne, where she won her first two gold medals. Her proudest moment came when she learned that her parents were at the pool watching her race. Friends and neighbors had given them money for their airfares.

Dawn Fraser went on to become the only swimmer to win gold medals at three Olympic Games in a row—a total of four gold medals. She was the first female swimmer to break one minute for the 100 meter freestyle, and she held the world 100 meter freestyle record for fifteen years. In her long career, Dawn Fraser set 39 world records.

DID YOU KNOW?

Dawn Fraser suffered from asthma all her life. Doctors believe that swimming is good exercise for asthma suffers. It was certainly good for Dawn!

Chapter 5
Muhammad Ali

When Muhammad Ali was 12 years old and growing up in Kentucky, someone stole his bike. He went to a nearby gym to ask for help. He saw men boxing and decided he would like to try it. He trained hard and after six weeks he won his first fight.

Muhammad Ali went on to become the greatest boxer of all time. At the 1960 Olympic Games in the United States, he won a gold medal for his country.

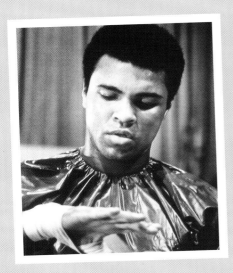

Ali's parents had named him Cassius Clay, but he changed his name to Muhammad Ali in 1964 at age 22. In that same year, he beat Sonny Liston to become the *heavyweight* champion of the world.

In 1974 Ali beat George Forman for the heavyweight title and showed the world he was still the greatest. He liked making up sayings. He told everyone: "I am the greatest. I float like a butterfly, sting like a bee."

Ali stopped boxing in 1979. He had won 56 fights with 37 knockouts. He lost only five times. He is the only boxer to win the world heavyweight title three times.

In 1984, Ali became sick with Parkinson's disease, but he still travels the world meeting his many fans.

? DID YOU KNOW?
Muhammad Ali used to tell people in which round he would win. When he boxed the British champion, Henry Cooper, he said he would win in round five, and he did.

Muhammad Ali was chosen to light the flame at the Olympic Games in Atlanta, 1996.

Chapter 6

Pele

When he was a young boy cleaning shoes in the streets of Brazil, Pele dreamed of playing soccer for his country.

A soccer coach saw Pele playing for a junior team, and he liked Pele's skills. When Pele turned 14, the coach took him to Santos, one of Brazil's most famous soccer clubs. He told the directors of the club: "This boy will be the greatest soccer player in the world."

Later that year, Pele played his first game for Santos and scored four goals.

Soon after his sixteenth birthday, Pele played his first game for Brazil and scored a goal.

In 1958, Pele played for Brazil in the World Cup in Sweden. He was a sensation! Brazil beat Sweden 5–2 in the final, and Pele scored two of the goals. His speed and skills made him popular all over the world.

By then, Pele was the greatest soccer player in the world. The fans loved him because he scored lots of goals. They also respected him because he was a fair player and a good sport. But he was also a player who helped his team mates on the field. They called him "the black pearl."

In 1975, Pele went to America to play for the New York Cosmos. Wherever he played, the fans enjoyed his incredible skills and respected his sense of fair play and good sportsmanship.

? DID YOU KNOW?
Pele was named Athlete of the Century in 1988. Pele played in four World Cups for Brazil, scoring twelve goals in 14 matches.

17

Chapter 7

Nadia Comaneci

Until Nadia Comaneci came along, no one had ever scored a perfect ten in a gymnastics competition. Nadia thrilled the fans at the 1976 Montreal Olympics when she scored a perfect ten, not once, but seven times.

When Nadia was six, a coach saw her doing gymnastics at school in Romania. The coach sent her to a special school for young gymnasts, where she trained in the gym for four hours every day. Her hard work was rewarded when she won the national junior titles in 1971 and 1972.

Nadia was 15 years old when she went to the Montreal Olympics and won three gold medals. At the 1980 Olympics in Moscow she won two more gold medals.

Nadia Comaneci achieved perfect scores because she could do very difficult exercises. She was the first woman to perform a double somersault from the *uneven parallel bars*.

After she retired in 1984, Nadia became a gymnastics judge and coach. She now lives in America.

? **DID YOU KNOW?**

When Nadia scored her seven perfect tens, she was only 4'8" tall and weighed just 86 pounds.

Chapter 8

Martina Navratilova

Like many champions, Martina Navratilova started practicing her sport when she was very young. When she was just four years old, Martina could hit a tennis ball up against a brick wall. By the time she was seven, she was already playing in tennis tournaments. She won the national championship of Czechoslovakia when she was 15.

Martina was born in Czechoslovakia, but later moved to the United States. Her first coach was her stepfather. He told her that she could become a famous tennis player. As they practiced together, he would call out to Martina, "Make believe you're at Wimbledon." Wimbledon is the most famous tennis championship in the world.

When Martina grew up, she won Wimbledon nine times. This is more than any other player. She also won every other major *tournament*. In her long career, Martina won 167 tournaments, which is more than any other tennis player, man or woman.

The
Navratilova
files

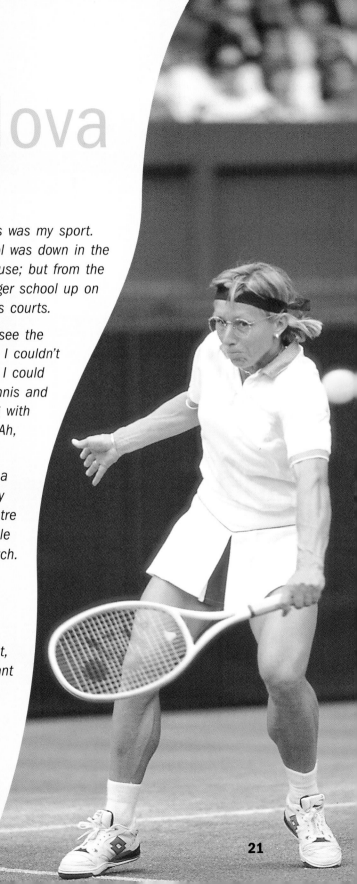

From the time I started school, tennis was my sport. From first grade to fifth grade, my school was down in the village square, a few blocks from our house; but from the sixth to the ninth grade, I went to a bigger school up on the hill, across the street from the tennis courts.

From my classroom windows I could see the courts and dream about being on them. I couldn't wait for cooking class to be finished, so I could run over there. The kids knew I loved tennis and they'd ask: "Martina, what are you doing with all this tennis?" And I'd think to myself, Ah, one day you'll know.

I already had an image of myself as a tennis player. It was formed the night my father took me to the Sparta sports centre in Prague, an arena where 10,000 people can watch a hockey game or tennis match. The big attraction that night was Rod Laver, the redheaded left-hander from Australia—the Rocket. What power and agility he had, what drive. I saw him rocketing around the court and I thought, That's it, that's me, that's the player I want to be. Women didn't play like him, not then, and not now, really, but if ever there was a player I wanted to copy, it was Laver.

Excerpt from *Being Myself* by Martina Navratilova and George Veesey, Collins, 1985.

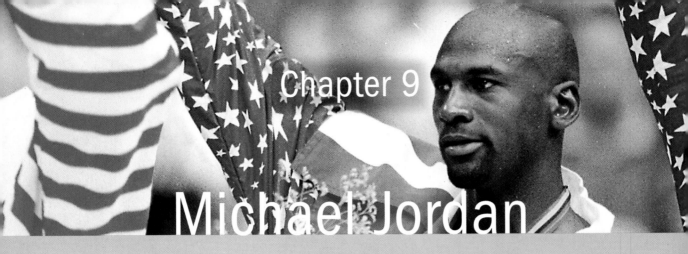

Chapter 9

Michael Jordan

Michael Jordan was always a winner at basketball. When he was in college, he scored the winning basket with only 13 seconds to play in the college championship final series.

After finishing college, he started playing for the Chicago Bulls. The Bulls were one of the worst teams in the conference when Michael joined them in 1984.

Later that year, he led the United States to the gold medal at the Olympic Games.

In 1991, the Bulls won the National Basketball Association title for the first time. He was chosen as the Most Valuable Player in the finals.

When his father died in 1993, Michael was so upset that he retired from basketball. He spent a lot of time with his family, and then he spent a season playing baseball with the Birmingham Barons team. He enjoyed playing baseball, but soon he realized that he liked basketball best.

? DID YOU KNOW?

In 1995, Michael Jordan went back to playing basketball with the Bulls. With Michael back on the team, the Bulls won their sixth NBA title in 1998. In the final game he scored the winning basket only five seconds before the end of the game. He then retired again.

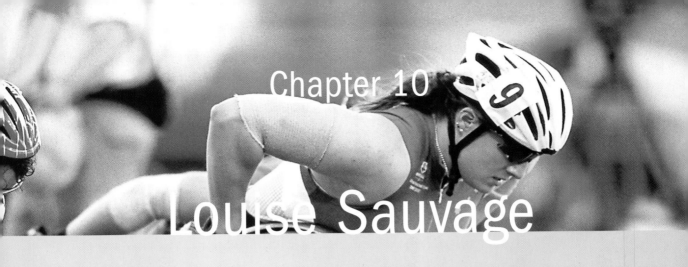

Chapter 10
Louise Sauvage

Louise Sauvage has competed at three *Paralympic Games*, winning nine gold medals. She has won the Boston Marathon three times. She was named International Sportswoman of the Year in 2000.

When Louise was young, she was told that a girl with a disability could never be a top athlete. She set out to prove that was wrong. Louise has shown people all over the world that even if you have a disability, you can still make your dreams come true. She has also shown that wheelchair sports can be exciting and fun. Her *motto* is "disabled kids need heroes too."

Louise has an intensive training program. This includes pushing her wheelchair more than 19 miles six mornings a week, lifting weights at the gym, and swimming and boxing to make her arms stronger. Wheelchair athletes need very strong arms so they can push their wheelchairs fast.

? DID YOU KNOW?
Wheelchair athletes use specially made wheelchairs called racing chairs. These chairs are longer than other wheelchairs. They have two back wheels and only one front wheel.

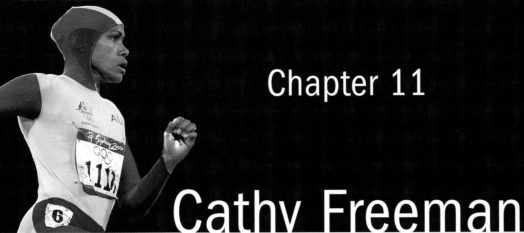

Chapter 11

Cathy Freeman

When Cathy Freeman won a gold medal in the 400 meter race at the 2000 Sydney Olympics, all Australians cheered. Several days earlier, at the opening ceremony, Cathy had the honor of lighting the Olympic flame in front of nearly 100,000 sports fans.

Cathy is the first indigenous Australian to win a gold medal in track and field at the Olympics. She had won a silver medal in the 400 meter at the Atlanta Olympics in 1996. In 1997, and again in 1999, she won the 400 meter at the World Championships. She is the first Australian to win two world athletic titles.

Cathy was born in Queensland in 1973. Her father was a champion rugby player and a fast runner. As a young girl, she showed that she, too, could run very fast and she won a scholarship to a boarding school where she was given professional coaching.

? DID YOU KNOW?

Cathy Freeman was selected as Young Australian of the Year in 1990 and Australian of the Year in 1998. She is the first person to receive both awards.

By the time she was 16, Cathy was selected to represent her country at the 1990 Commonwealth Games, where she won a gold medal in the 4 x 100 meter relay. She promised herself that one day she would win a gold medal at the Olympics. Ten years later, in Sydney, her dream came true.

How does Cathy do it? "I love running. I love competing. It's really simple," she says.

Chapter 1

Ian Thorpe

In the first two days of the Sydney 2000 Olympics, 17 year-old Ian Thorpe collected two gold medals in the swimming, winning the 400 meter freestyle and the 4 x 100 meter freestyle relay. When he won the 400 meter, Ian broke his own world record. He finished the games with three gold and two silver medals and carried the flag for Australia at the closing ceremony.

At only 14, Ian became the youngest male swimmer to be selected for an Australian swimming team. The following year he became the youngest world champion when he won the 400 meter freestyle at the World Championships.

Ian, who was born in Sydney, started swimming when he was eight years old after watching his older sister train at the local pool. Although he started swimming backstroke, he soon switched to freestyle.

His coach says Ian is the hardest trainer he has ever seen. Hard work is one reason why Ian is a champion. Another is the length of his arms. With his arms outstretched they span 74" from finger tips to finger tips—almost 10" longer than other boys his age. This allows him to swim 6½ feet every second he is in the pool.

In other swimming championships, Ian won four gold medals and broke three world records.

Ian's biggest fans are his parents. They have watched all his races since he started swimming.

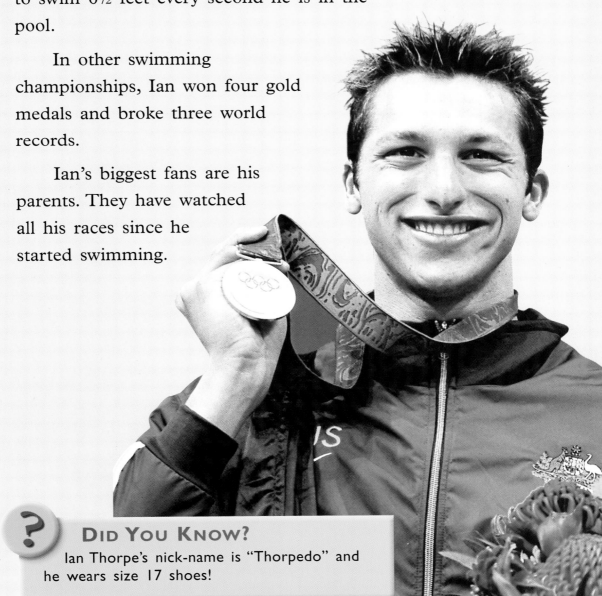

Chapter 13

Are You a Hero?

Think about the athlete you admire most. Why do you admire this person? Now imagine that you are very good at a sport. In which sport would you like to be a hero? What type of special skills would you need? You might need to be very quick, like a short-distance runner, or very determined like a marathon runner. What sort of training do you think you would have to do?

Just imagine: you could be a sports hero for thousands of people around the world.

Sir Donald Bradman

Carl Lewis

Steve Redgrave

Kieren Perkins

Karrie Webb

Marion Jones

Mark McGuire

Glossary

autograph	when a famous person signs his or her name for a fan
freestyle	a type of swimming stroke
heavyweight	this is the category for boxers who weigh more than 175 pounds
motto	a saying
Paralympic Games	an international sports competition for disabled athletes
professional	when someone is paid for playing a sport
tournament	a sport competition
uneven parallel bars	in gymnastics, these are two bars that are parallel to each other, but at different heights